The Forgiveness Letters

Shiarnice Taylor

In Loving Memory of

Mary "MAMA" Hazel Richard, my Great Grandmother

You will truly be missed. We love you!!

Rest in Heaven

Sunrise: March 21st 1928- Sunset: September 15, 2017 @ 3pm

<u>The Strongest Woman We Knew</u>

"We are of good courage, I say, and are willing rather to be absent, and to be at home with the Lord." 2 Corinthians 5:8.

What shall we say then when our hearts long for Peace that we can't find?

When strength turns into weakness because our courage is gone?

When tears roll down our cheeks like tides rolling over sand?

When our love can't be laid to rest and taken to Heaven and we have no more days on this Earth with our Beloved Mother, Grandmother, the strongest woman we knew but human strength can't prevail over God's will and plan.

On this beloved day we cried out in the flesh but rejoiced in spirit exalting the life of Mary Hazel Richard, a truly remarkable Samaritan of Fortitude and Favor.

God saw fit to bless her with 13 children and grant her 89 extraordinary years on this Earth.

I've heard the voices of angels nominate her as The Strongest Woman they knew, and a consensus on Earth that she was the greatest inspiration to her children, grandchildren and women.

Righteously choosing to live, she grabbed onto the ropes of life and held tightly onto the remnants of hope until she was ready; YES, when she was ready to let go and let God set her free! Home is where she desired to be.

While there was air in her lungs there was purpose in her pain a permanent halo surrounding her from beginning to end? God saw fit to allow her story and legacy to set a record and trend.

When we have no words to describe the courage we need to ask God to bring us out of our grief, we can look to her because her strength is what speaks to the essence of our hearts.

An electrifying spirit, she was an excellent zydeco dancer, twirling circles of kindness around strangers where everything she touched seemed to radiate with God's Grace. A meek and gentle spirit, it seemed she never had a bad day as she displayed what it looks like to not complain but always having a smile on your face. There was purpose behind her pain, always an indication that she knew who you were and what you possessed. She saw through our souls and made us better people.

Peace never looked better on anyone, and she was dressed in it from head to toe. She found joy in the simple things of life – family, crossword puzzles, and (teaching us that the simple things in life matter more than overthinking complicated situations). She would rather breathe life into something than to waste breathe on lifeless quarrels.

She wore the fruit of the spirit as her crown displaying each of them seemingly effortless:

Love - Her love was unconditional

Joy - Her joy was remarkable

Peace - Her Peace was insightful

Her Self-Discipline was masterful.

Her Kindness was gravitating.

Her Goodness was righteous.

Her Faithfulness was unmeasured.

Her Gentleness was delicate.

Her long suffering was unmerited but with direction, hope, and resolve.

The Strongest Woman We Knew has been coined as the new phrase for us all to aspire to be!!

There will never be another Mary Hazel "Mama" Richard. We are fortunate to have known you and grateful that God loaned you to us for what seemed never long enough but within God's perfect plan we accept the challenge from Heaven to rise to greatness as she would have wanted. We mourn and remember The Strongest Woman We Knew, and somewhere in Heaven to a Keith Frank Zydeco tune you are dancing, dancing away.

Dance, MAMA, Dance!!

Table of Contents

Part 1

Forgiving Family

Part 2

Forgiving Friends

Part 3

Forgiving Circumstances

Part 4

Forgiving God

Prologue

One of the most valuable acts we can offer one another is forgiveness, as it is the cornerstone of the Christian Faith and it stands as the gate of salvation next to Grace. It is vital, yet in our carnal bodies and minds it is difficult to do. No one, not a soul, was created perfect. However; the harsh reality that we face is that forgiveness is something we must do if we want Christ to forgive our sins. Whether we lie, gossip, fornicate, adulterate, shack up, murder, get drunk, or we live our lives in unforgiveness, we must understand that all of these are sins. Forgiveness takes time, and God has a plan for his provision. We oftentimes tell God what our timeline will be before we forgive someone. When, if you pray to God to work on softening your heart, he will begin to break the mold and chip away at the real issues you have with that someone you cannot seem to forgive. It is at that point your timeline for forgiveness will become inapplicable.

I invite you to follow me on this journey of forgiveness by experiencing how to forgive, how to ask God to open your heart to forgive, how to extend grace, how to love again, how to love people as God has loved us. This journey will provide you real life human examples of how difficult, but necessary forgiveness is by incorporating the use of letters and poetry to exhibit true forgiveness.

Forgiving Mama

Mama, I haven't always liked your taste in men nor your passive nature. How you seem to just let things happen, never reacting, just settling. Perhaps I never stopped to realize that settling to me was always your normal.

I never sought to understand or even stopped to think about what you may have had to endure. Growing up without your father must have been hard, and while I don't know much about your high school life, from what I've heard it seemed that it was rough. Seemed you had had enough of seizures and anxiety, and demeaning relationships appeared to dominate your life.

Keep in mind this is only my guess based on pieces of stories I've heard from your past experiences. We never talked about these things. We never talked about menstrual cycles, what settling looked like, about how to do make-up, or even about sex. I can admit I blamed you partially for my own promiscuity. I blamed you for never showing me what I was worth and how it took me so long to find out I was worth more than a dime. Truth is, I never bothered to ask you if you knew your worth, if you were tired of men cheating on you; tired of experiencing emotional abuse, tired of coming home to another brick in the window or a keyed-up car. Please forgive me. These are only recollections and reflections of what some of my childhood looked like. I never blamed you for my father not being there, but I blamed you for not believing in his change. Now I see why you didn't believe in his change because he wasn't changing. I never felt like you didn't love me. At times I felt like you loved the wrong men more than me, but now I see because of your absent father maybe you were searching for love just like I searched for my father. Always seeking approval from my father, but he was never around to get it. We both never got an opportunity to be daddy's little girl, yet your father played father to all his other children. I never thought how that might have made you feel, so forgive me for ignoring that part of your life. Forgive me for not acknowledging what you did right. You raised me on your own from your 16th birthday to my first birthday. I'm now two years from turning 30 and your name is still the first name next to God that I call on. You worked to make sure I ate, had clothes on my back and name brand shoes on my feet. You always had high expectations that I get a good education. You pushed me, even when I didn't want to go to private school. You saw the shine in me. You comforted me in sadness when my father would make broken promises to pick me up. You always made sure I knew I was loved, and you found a way to make sure we always had fun. With limited resources, you always found a way to celebrate all my accomplishments - from graduation to track meets, to street Olympics to basketball, volleyball, and poetry – {you gently pushed me into excellence} uplifted me. You created a masterpiece, and I went on to get my Masters' Degree. You encouraged me, allowing me to never settle.

At points in my life when I felt as though I could never talk to you about topics that weren't popular between mother and daughters, it still becomes a little awkward between us discussing relationship matters. But God gave me the courage to approach every topic that seemed off limits and you seemed to get me. You were relatable, you were discrete, you were an amazing counselor in my times of need. You comforted me during my mess and collected all my trash and turned it into treasure. You rebuilt me, with God's help and I knew there was nothing I couldn't tell you - my MAMA. There was no level of disappointment I couldn't come back from. You were and are my MAMA, and I hope you can forgive me for never understanding the who, what, when, where, why and how of my upbringing. I have come to realize you did the best you could, and you did an AMAZING JOB with what God blessed you with. Forgive me for being angry with you for years and trying to force my life onto yours and never accepting your reality as your normal. Forgive me for trying to parent you and teach you how to parent my brother. Hopefully I will understand once I have my own children what it takes to be the parent of a young black boy. I'm now learning what you meant by sometimes it's just better to let things go. Now I understand why you are so passive. In fact, it's not that you are passive as much as it is you choose to live in peace verses chaos. Life is too short, and I'm working on modeling that aspect of my life after you.

Letter to Mama

I write this 2nd letter in knowledge and curiosity, in hopes to get to know you better. I write this letter in admiration of the woman you have become because of what you've gone through. I write it in true submission to God, because in my selfishness I would have never admitted that I needed to forgive you and that you needed to forgive me.

I write it because I'm tired of sweeping the truth under a rug that no longer will lay flat on the floor because there is so much stuff under there that now it just looks like a big tarp covering an old car.

I write this because I love you, and unconditional love doesn't hold back. At one point, I was angry and confused by your life; by the life you chose for us because every man you decided to be with affected me and my brother greatly. It seemed as if everything you touched was cursed because I never heard your voice. It was like your life was stuck somewhere under your heart.

I never understood that being passive was really your way of depriving yourself from worrying too much. It seemed at times that you were willing to let others walk over you just so that you could walk around fear, anxiety, and depression.

Mama, I'm sorry I never understood you. I apologize for never taking the time to understand the genealogy of the generational curses in our lives. I never even asked you how much your father not being a part of your life resembled so much of the same pattern of my father not being there. You only chose what was familiar to you.

Optimistic and hopeful like me you must have been. We are so much alike. I've come to understand the saying of when two people that are so much alike they tend not to get along. I now see the resemblance, not just on our faces, but in our circumstances.

I'm sorry for never taking the time to acknowledge the work you put in to make sure me and my brother had everything we needed; sometimes more than we needed. I'm sorry for penalizing you for giving him more than me. I didn't see that what you gave him was what you felt I lacked and what you lacked as a child. You were only making up for decades of lost stuff, and I blamed you for giving him more stuff. More materialistic items that could never mend his broken heart of his father being in prison nearly all his life. At times it seemed that you ruined him, but now I see my brother for who he is - the man that is nothing like his father and everything like you. He is loving, caring, compassionate; a fighter but only when he has to be. He is a diligent worker, willing to accept criticism. He's never been afforded the opportunity to put his all into anything he picks up with his hands. I have you and God to thank for that and me thinking that your hands could never mold him into a man. I owe you an apology.

My disbelief and distrust shows just how much credit I was willing to give you even though I felt you made the wrong choices in the men you dated. You chose to mold the right man, my brother. This man you have made great, even though so many other men never made you great.

They never understood your value like I see you now. Even still, your value is buried under oceans of responsibility, under unreleased potential, under landmines of settling. But maybe that's just my perception of your reality when in fact your reality is possibly a lot more blissful than I make it out to be.

I'm sorry, mama, that I tried to run your life how I wanted my life to be. Yet you never tried to run my life and turn me into you.

You always wanted me to reach this place as a woman, and I know you always chose the right side verses the latter. For that I thank you for being an amazing mother.

We don't understand each other sometimes, but all we have to do is look at one another and see a reflection of ourselves. My resemblance to my father turned into my resemblance of you because God wanted me to see that the mother I blamed for my past mistakes was the same mother that wanted to protect me from all of it.

I'm sorry, mama; for not believing in you enough, and for it taking me so long to see you! For it taking me so long to see your heart!

Your love for me!

Your desires for me!

I'm sorry it took me so long to say I accept you the way you are and all that you come with because all of it is what makes you you! All of it is what makes you my mama and I wouldn't trade you for anything in the world.

I pray you accept my apologies and continue to show your

grace towards me as I will continue to share with you.

Love your only daughter,

Shiarnice Taylor

Forgiving Daddy

The hardest thing I've had to do was forgive you. It becomes even harder when you continue to make promises that you can't keep. It's like repentance, where every time you do something new I have to go back to the drawing board and remind myself that I can't hold your past hostage. I have to remind myself that everything new that you've done to hurt me has to still be forgiven. Forgiving you has taught me how to extend grace to others.

I used to hate how you would lie to me, how you would manipulate me into believing that you were changing even though you weren't; how you took credit for my successes although you had no part in parenting me. I learned the most from you the Summer 2005 when you came home from prison I was 16 and went to live with grandma. In every letter you promised you would be a better father and told me you wanted me to come and stay with you a while for us to spend time together. I remember that summer vividly. The Jamie Foxx album, Unpredictable, had just come out. I remember you picking me up and listening to "Blame it on the Alcohol." I remember the wind blowing in my hair, putting my arms out the window of your new Chrysler 300 thinking how amazing it felt to be with you. I thought you were so cool. You seemed very popular with the ladies. It appeared you had this charm that could lure anybody into liking you.

That entire summer I felt free and liberated from the tight reigns my mom had on me, which later I understood that discipline served a purpose. You let me do anything I wanted to do that summer. I witnessed you woo and wine and dine all types of women, telling them you loved them only to ignore their phone calls later.

The most disturbing part of that summer was when you brought home a woman who was obviously high on drugs and she looked just like me. She was high and aloof to where she was, and I remember you saying, "Hey baby girl, doesn't this woman look just like you?" I was 16 years old and didn't completely understand why I was so disturbed. Why did my skin crawl when you two went into the room and the lights went off and didn't come back on for several hours? I can only guess what occurred in that room, and the only thing I could remember is thinking to myself that if this woman looked just like me (which she did), how perverted that was; how sick you must be to want to have sex with a woman who was lost, high and looked just like your

16-year-old daughter. I hated you for that day, and at that moment I wanted to go back home and never live with you again.

What was hard was trying to understand your logic all those years in why you never came to any of my graduations; how I stood by the door with my overnight bag waiting for you to pick me up and you never came. Trying to understand how you would lie on other people to cover up your mistakes. Trying to understand how you could let your daughter starve while in college and have me drive all the way to Houston from Huntsville using my last money for gas to come and get money from you for food then use your wife as a scapegoat to tell me you had no money. I never understood how you could come up to my school while I was a freshman in college and hear my friends telling me how cute you were and how they wanted to sleep with you (I was so disgusted by that). You bragging about how young you looked and how you could pull anyone of those college women. No matter how much I hated you and blamed you for my own promiscuity and problems of self-worth, I had to face reality and understand that at some point I couldn't blame you anymore.

You want to know what's crazy? The expectation that people will change based on your own perception of where you see the potential of where they need to be. What is even crazier than continuing to do the same thing and expecting a different outcome is seeing someone's potential and believing you can change them based on your standard of where you see them going. My father has not accepted his faults and possibly never will. However, what does that have to do with me? If you noticed, forgiveness is not about him ultimately understanding his faults as much as it is about seeking freedom for oneself. This part I call apologizing to daddy (which seems insane, after all he's done to me). It is important to understand that there is no forgiveness without Grace and there is no Grace without forgiveness. Grace and Mercy are the essential tools, like pen and paper is necessary to write, Grace and Mercy are necessary and precedes forgiveness. Ephesians 2:3-9 states, "Like the rest, we were by nature deserving of wrath. But because of his great love for us, God, who is rich in mercy, made us alive with Christ even when we were dead in transgressions - it is by grace you have been saved. And God raised us up with Christ and seated us with him in the heavenly realms in Christ Jesus, in order that in coming ages he might show the incomparable riches of his grace, expressed in his kindness to us in Christ Jesus. For it is by grace you have been saved, through faith-and this is not from yourselves, it is the gift of God - not by works, so that no one can boast."

My father deserves grace and mercy just as I do. I can't expect God to show me grace if I am not willing to extend grace to my father, my neighbor, strangers or anyone for that matter. Going to church every Sunday, singing in the choir, serving in ministries, nor paying my tithes and offering can make me look no more presentable to God when I continuously harbor resentment in my heart for my father's past actions. It is time to make the first move and apologize.

•

Father, daddy, I apologize for never accepting {the essence of who you are} who you were truly. There are still aspects of you that I don't know and I'm sure wonderful aspects of who you are that I have not had a chance to get to know. I am sorry that I wasted time focusing on the negative aspects of your character instead of uplifting and encouraging the positive experiences that we shared, such as you coming to my Masters graduation ceremony. I apologize for taking so long to forgive you and never taking the time to understand the neighborhood you grew up in; whether your own father's passing (when you were so young) impacted you negatively and didn't teach you how to be a Father. I apologize for the preconceived notions that I often still have about the belief that you cannot or will not change. I want you to know that I now believe in the power of Jesus Christ and the ability for any man to change. II Corinthians 5:17 tells us that "…any man in Christ is a new creation, old things are passed away {and all things become new}"

I'm not sure if you are a Christian, but above all, in forgiveness I offer you my Faith, sharing with you Christ. I pray every day that you will {accept Christ as your Savior} become saved even if it's not through me introducing you to Christ. I apologize for never introducing you to Christ through my actions and my walk. I apologize for deciding to close the door on our relationship, never checking on you to see where you are in life. I apologize for acting better than you, as though I was on another level somehow because I am saved. I apologize for my assumptions that you aren't saved. I apologize for trying to become a part of your life even though you decided not to become a part of my life. The Bible instructs us to honor thy mother and thy father, and so I apologize for not honoring you and showing you the respect you deserve no matter what your actions were towards me. I apologize for not loving you at moments in my life where I was ashamed of you and wanted to hide and even sometimes wanting to change my last name. I understand now that our predispositions to bad parenting doesn't predestine who we are nor what we will become. I recognize God's awesome power to change people.

Lastly, I apologize for expecting God to give me Grace when I never extended grace to you. I pray you can accept my apology.

Sincerely Your Oldest Daughter,

Shiarnice Taylor

<u>**Grace**</u>

If Grace be the same prayer that we both pray before and after meals, then it is clear that we say, 'Thank you' after meals when our Flesh has been fed and our spirit only receives happy meals now that it grace after the pain he heals so that's the after feeling called conviction did you remember to Thank Him before he granted you Grace? Or were too afraid of what others would think or say?

Better yet did you remember that sacrifice and obedience is better than a godless heart don't get it twisted grace is free, but it doesn't give you the permission to forget to listen it seems your spiritual cancer is in remission not that's spelled FAITH don't use your obedience as your last option, but you'd rather phone a friend first rather than Listen to a God that gave you your worth.

If Grace be the same thing as receiving a reprieve even after being late to work several times and avoiding the consequences of being fired, I would hate to see the man who hired the man who can do the ultimate firing. God chose to extend his unmerited favor as manifested in the Salvation of sinners like you and me, yet we keep running across that line to see what it would take to make an inch grow into six feet deep. Even as you remind your flesh that the wages of sin is death, but you keep dancing with the devil; keep asking the bank for a loan that you know you can't pay back, asking for an extension even as he keeps handing out Grace periods.

When will enough be enough, and what if God stopped handing out Grace Period?!!! What if the vehicle that drives your Faith, that extends Grace, ran out of giving you favors and all privileges of Mercy are now revoked all of a sudden repossessed?

A criminal can commit a crime and receive probation based on what is called Deferred Adjudication, allowing one to be free. It gives one an advocate, a decency unlike the nature of us Humans. Can you extend such amazing Grace is a courtesy of politeness excusing some of the biggest mistakes that we all make? Oh, the Righteousness of our God!

Did you really learn your lesson when you cheated on your wife all those times and still she stayed? Or how about all those times when the Holy Spirit called your name as you lay down in the sweat of your conviction, sinful epidemics, testing the walls of Grace only to be left with the paranoia of is she pregnant? Did he give me something that I can't get rid of? What saved your life is the same thing that you prayed for when you put your hands together to pray before and after your meals. So, let us say Grace one last time to give you permission to go ahead and commit that sin once more and again.

It seems you got it twisted and thought your blessings outweighed your consequences when it was not your works that saved you. Even if you put in the work, no matter how much you made or how much you prayed, it will never amount to something that God gives us for free. Can you see you are testing a patient God, a waiting God, an 'Oh I'll send you some mercy now and you just thank Him later God, even though you don't deserve it loving God?'

That same Grace that was extended to Jonah, Paul, Daniel, Job; given to the Egyptians and Joseph while in Prison, Shadrach, Meshach and Abednego in a fiery furnace. God is our spiritual hope, but saying grace before a meal in front of our coworkers is way too much.

I'm so tired of us using grace as a spiritual crutch, an excuse to wear make-up even though we know we got all kinds of ugly on the inside. We use it as an excuse to schedule sin on our calendars and feel bad this one time but plan to do it over and over again. Using grace as a friendship of utility but that doesn't mean we ain't got responsibilities. What shall we say then? Shall we continue to live in sin so that Grace may increase? We think this because Grace is free. But the Apostle Paul tells us that by no means can we who died to sin live it in any longer. How can a pig continue to wallow in a mud full of mess? Maybe we can be compared to pigs or dumb sheep. How much longer will you pretend to be asleep to use the excuse that I'll keep on sinning because Grace is free.

But I forgot some pigs enjoy wallowing in their own mess!!

Letter to my Brother

Lulu, Papa, Red Skeleton, sweet baby brother:

You are not so little anymore. Although I always wished I could protect you from the injustices in this world, I knew I couldn't. As your big sister, I felt the extreme responsibility of filling the shoes that your Father never filled for you.

I always had the desire to show you that the life that proceeded you will be safe and secure. I would be able to provide you with all possible outcomes of a better life, shielding you by creating faith and salvation for you.

I pray that you will always be cradled in the arms of Christ when you feel alone and misunderstood; that if no one knows what you are feeling when you feel as though your father {doesn't?} exist, know that your true Father in Heaven exists. You are not alone!

I want you to know that it makes no sense to apologize for the gender I was born in, but I'll apologize anyway because if I were your Father I wouldn't just say I love you I would show you!!

I'd go to every baseball and football game you ever played.

I'd go to every boxing match.

I'd go to every parent/ teacher conference to ensure your grades and behavior were where they should be.

I'd call you every day to ensure you are making sound decisions and I'd make you go to church every Sunday and even on Wednesday nights just to make sure your salvation is solidified in Christ and that you know God for yourself.

I'd meet all your friends to make sure they were people of good character and not knuckle heads allowing you to get in trouble.

But because I am only your sister and the capacity of my responsibility over you only extends so far

I'd first apologize for putting so many boyfriends before you.

I'd admit to you that over the years I was selfish and felt like because I was still finding myself and felt alone because my dad wasn't there I wasn't fully the sibling I should be for you.

I'd apologize to you for trying to make you into me, for setting the bar sometimes so high that it seemed unreachable and created unrealistic expectations of who you should be for you and not for me, our mom or anyone else.

I'd encourage you to always be yourself and not be a follower.

I have and always will encourage you to talk to me about any and everything, never feeling as though you can't talk to me because I am your big sister. I won't always have all the answers, but I will never make the mistake creating a barrier between us.

I will never shield you from what is reality in this world and I'll never apologize for sharing with you real life experiences that I've faced to make you a better person.

My everlasting prayer for you is that you will come to know God for yourself and I will pray that prayer until you finally break down and accept that you are a child of God.

God loves you so much and because you have a calling and purpose over your life the devil wants to tear you down. The devil wants you to be another statistic, but God wants you to be a leader, a loving compassionate, strong-willed man of God. God wants you to know that although your father wasn't there, God is all the Father you will ever need!!

I pray you find peace and joy in this letter and ultimately salvation to be the man Christ desires for you to be.

I love you and hope you will accept my apology for not pushing you harder. You deserve a constant challenge!!

Your Big Sis,

Shiarnice Taylor

Letter to my Sister

"The Price of anything is the amount of life you exchange for it."

-Henry David Thoreau

To my sister: I want you to live.

I want you to know how much I love you and how much God loves you.

How you are worth so much more than anybody putting you through so much.

You are beautiful, smart, a great mother and filled with purpose.

There is so much that God has in store for you and I pray you get to experience all that life has to offer.

Don't give on up life!

Your Kids need you!

Your family need you!

God needs you to live so he allowed you to still be here.

Take life by the hand and never let it go, ever again for anyone.

Don't let anyone make you feel as though you don't have the right to live.

You have never had a problem attracting any man God will send you someone that will love you and your children unconditionally.

Love is someone caring for you more than themselves.

Love is someone laying down their life for you and if they wouldn't they don't love you.

I love you and I want you to live for as long as God wants you here.

I'm sorry for closing the door and failing you as your sister.

I apologize for not staying around because of petty gossip that has no place now.

I want to be present in my niece and nephew's life.

I want you to know that closing the door on you was never about anything I could prove you did. Nothing excuses the fact that I wasn't there for you!

As your big sister it was important for me to show you a better example of what a woman of God looks like and I failed to do that so I'm sorry.

I pray I'll have that opportunity again, when you are ready.

Don't give up on life and never let anyone make you give up!!

You deserve to live!

Sincerely Your Big Sis,

Shiarnice Taylor

(P.S. These are all the things I always wanted to say but never had the opportunity to tell you and I pray one day you will be ready to receive them.)

<u>**Her life Matters**</u>

She is beautiful from the crown of her head to the soles of her feet; her soul emits radiance ebony pearls grace her waist her face is illuminated shining only in darkness she is the salt and light of every ground she traipse.

She is radiant in all her Glory she is the poem and the story of a Nikki Giovanni's egotripping authority she demands respect and often people confuse her standards with an unpleasant demeanor she just refuses to let any man demean her

She is eminent, divine, and refined like a ammolite the processes of finding her requires tunneling through some of her insecurities, past and present sins even some traumatic events but it's worth unearthing what God calls a good thing she been talked about, ridiculed, spat upon her backbone is fragmented and her help has been unappreciated who is she you might ask?

She is a black woman suffocating under the rubble of an enslaved mindset called America, she is the yoke joining together an entire Kingdom of visionaries she sees potential germinating inside of a black man

She is the Coretta to his Kingdom

She is the Hope of Michelle Obama

The Courage of Ruby Bridges

The tenacity of Rosa Parks

The Faith of Evelyn Lowery

The Organization of Daisy Bates

The Fire of Nina Simone

The Stride of Jackie Joyner-Kersee

And Stories of Zora Neal-Hurston

She is self-less and she understands that she cannot just accept anybody because she is more than somebody that doesn't belong to everybody she belongs to a King therefore she should be adorned as a Black Queen

She is not perfect but always working to be better

She is an Ebony enigma of a woman and proud to say that her life matters.

Forgiving Friends

Forgiving my 9th grade Best friend

God gives us two commandments that we must follow. Love God with all your heart and love thy neighbor as thyself. I love God too much to allow my unforgiveness and anger to control me any longer. God commands us to love others and therefore because there is no such thing in the bible as like and dislike: we either hate or we love. I know for a fact I don't hate you I love you and have wished the best for you since the incident that occurred nearly almost 2 years ago. I cannot allow human emotion anymore to dominate my life. I need to say this to you and the only way I knew to do it without making a big deal or allowing anyone on social media to step in and keep this between me and you was through a letter. It was the most appropriate way. This letter is not intended to rehash what happened and blame you for anything; however, it is to explain what I did wrong and give you an opportunity to contact me to express to me how I made you feel and hopefully you will accept my apology and whatever God has in store for the both of us; hopefully we can move past this and continue with our lives and not be held back any longer. A problem is never resolved by non-communication, in fact a problem never magically gets solved. It takes someone stepping forward, taking the first step towards reconciliation and resolution. I want to first apologize for assuming you knew what occurred that night. I want to apologize for expecting you to take sides during a difficult time where so many times you were always caught in the middle of allot of discord. I want to apologize for sending you the picture of my face expecting you to know how angry I was or even understand when I can't be sure you saw what happened. I want to apologize for even going to New Orleans as God told me a week prior not to go and I ignored his request and went anyway. My disobedience to God caused everything to transpire. I want to apologize for putting you in harm when I decided that my only recourse was to pull a gun in which I thought would save my life, but now know I could have made a better decision. I want to apologize for drinking so much and not being coherent enough to understand or know what I would do or say when something like that occurred. I want to apologize only for what occurred that night, how I treated you afterwards, and how my family treated you. Things could have happened differently. It has been difficult for me to trust people since then, but to build new relationships and friendships I have to ask for forgiveness and forgive those who I feel hurt me. I was hurt and angered from both you and Alicia; however, that doesn't change what I did, and it didn't help. It only escalated the situation. I plan on sending the same letter to Alicia and hope to obtain her forgiveness as well and just because you forgive someone it doesn't mean you have to be my friend or give me a 2nd chance or 3rd chance or anything. All forgiveness does is allow us to reconcile and know we can move past this with a clean slate. It allows us to move on in life and become better people knowing we aren't holding grudges against anyone. Our past has held me hostage for too long and I don't know about you, but I won't repeat the mistakes my family has made by just sweeping things under the rug and hoping they go away that doesn't work. I can't truly say what happened that night. We were all having a good time and things just turned for the worst. I saw the worst in me and understand that had I shot Alicia she wouldn't be here for son or her family. I would have gone to prison, no matter self-defense or whatever I claimed it was. I could have lost everything, and they could have lost everything and so could you being associated with me, putting you in an unsafe place and I'm sorry for that. God's grace is so amazing and to be alive and well is so much more important that harboring anger and resentment towards you. I hope we can all share with one another what went wrong and move on with our lives and pray God's will prevails in our lives. I'm not perfect and I never will be. Our friendship in the past was very shaky and if I were you I wouldn't trust me either, but one thing about me that has never changed is that I love hard and my love for Christ is stronger than my hate for anyone. You may never trust me again or even respond to this letter, but at least I know I extended forgiveness and an apology to you sincerely and I tried my best to resolve this matter. It is up to you to accept or reject. I don't hate you or Alicia and why should I? I have no reason to hate anyone God has blessed me tremendously and I am nothing but grateful. I apologize for making you sad, angry, frustrated, and whatever other emotions I took you through when you read my text. My approach was horrible, and I had just experienced the most traumatic thing in my life; however, you were not to blame nor was Alicia. We shouldn't have even gone, and I faced consequences for what God told me not to do.

I pray this finds you well and successful and happy, loving, trusting and open again and not hindered by any of this. I also hope you respond to this by sending me an email back to

ShiarniceTaylor@yahoo.com. I didn't want to put an address as I will be moving soon, but I would like to hear from you about how I made

you feel, and what I did, and you can be as mean and real and

completely honest. I'm ready for all of it, whatever names you want to

call me or not I'm ok with it. It's nothing I haven't been called before

and at one point they represented who I was, but not anymore because

GOD can change anybody!! So, I hope you respond to this and forgive

me and my response will only be when you respond I'm sorry again

nothing more nothing less I don't want to add to conflict I just want it

resolved and to move on with our lives.

Sincerely,

Shiarnice Taylor

Letter to my college/poetry Best friend

1 John 4:7-21New International Version (NIV)

[7] Dear friends, let us love one another, for love comes from God. Everyone who loves has been born of God and knows God. [8] Whoever does not love does not know God, because God is love. [9] This is how God showed his love among us: He sent his one and only Son into the world that we might live through him. [10] This is love: not that we loved God, but that he loved us and sent his Son as an atoning sacrifice for our sins.[11] Dear friends, since God so loved us, we also ought to love one another.[12] No one has ever seen God; but if we love one another, God lives in us and his love is made complete in us.

[13] This is how we know that we live in him and he in us: He has given us of his Spirit. [14] And we have seen and testify that the Father has sent his Son to be the Savior of the world. [15] If anyone acknowledges that Jesus is the Son of God, God lives in them and them in God. [16] And so we know and rely on the love God has for us.

God is love. Whoever lives in love lives in God, and God in them. [17] This is how love is made complete among us so that we will have confidence on the day of judgment: In this world we are like

Jesus. [18] There is no fear in love. But perfect love drives out fear, because fear has to do with punishment. The one who fears is not made perfect in love.

[19] We love because he first loved us. [20] Whoever claims to love God yet hates a brother or sister is a liar. For whoever does not love their brother and sister, whom they have seen, cannot love God, whom they have not seen. [21] And he has given us this command: Anyone who loves God must also love their brother and sister.

I want to start out by saying I love you. If I don't love you, I cannot say I love God. This letter is intended to express what I was unable to say two years ago and extend also my forgiveness from the apology you tried to give me after everything happened. This letter is not intended to point fingers at who was wrong or intended to blame anyone further for pain we both suffered during that night in New Orleans. I know I am not your favorite person in the world that you expected to hear from, but I find it necessary to forgive and ask that you forgive me for things that I didn't realize were wrong then, but now I do, and I need to apologize. I apologize, first and foremost for being disobedient for still deciding to go to New Orleans even when God requested that I not go. I ignored signs, feelings of uneasiness knowing there was a reason we shouldn't be there in the first place. I recognize that my disobedience to God and listening to the Holy Spirit has caused a lot of turmoil in my life. In addition, it placed us in a situation in which we all were unsafe and irrational. I apologize for ignoring the fact that you at the time did have responsibilities such as school, a son, financial obligations, and my selfishness, in wanting to have fun during my birthday caused unnecessary strains in your life that could have been avoided. I neglected you and your son and out of my selfishness, whether intoxicated or not. I decided to defend myself in the most detrimental way, not realizing the consequences of my actions, which could have caused a temporary situation to turn into something permanent. You could have been permanently removed from this Earth, not only from your family, but from your son. I apologize for such desperate measures that were taken to defend myself. It was irrational and could have been handled in a different manner.

I felt invincible with a weapon, which is why I haven't bought another weapon since that incident. I have been consistently reevaluating the consequences of what it means to shoot someone and possibly be in prison. I apologize for drinking so much to where my judgement was clouded, and I was unable to make better logical decisions than to physically fight you, not recognizing that we both had so much to lose and it wasn't worth it. I understand the hate you and your family may have for me, but this letter is not to focus on the emotion of hate, but to focus on the action of love and how my absence of love towards you is one that needs to be apologized for. I apologize for not accepting your apology the first time in New Orleans. I was in such shock and disbelief of my actions and yours that it did not register to me to remember all the years of our friendship and listen to you and your sincere apology. I do offer my forgiveness now although I couldn't offer it back then. I apologize for the actions of my family influencing my decision to choose not to allow you to ride back with me causing your parents to have to spend money to have you flown back to Houston. My distrust for you and my safety were the only important factors to me to ensure more damage wasn't done. I failed to make my own decision as an adult; whether I chose to let you ride back with me or not it was a decision as an adult I should have made and not allowed my family to cloud my judgement. I apologize for ignoring your safety, now realizing that your safety was at risk more than my own was. Deciding to point a gun in your direction was one of the worst decisions I have ever made.

The moment I pointed that gun at you, I heard the Holy Spirit loud and clear that day screaming "Don't do it! She has a son". I apologize because, to be honest, all I thought about was your son and how much I loved him and how the permanent decision to shoot that weapon could have ended in him losing you. The love I have for him would have been completely null and void, because if I have so much love for him then I should have so much more respect and love for his mother. All the years you were there for me supporting me from poetry shows to graduation and the love and trust I had for you disappeared that night; but true forgiveness changes those results.

Forgiving each other allows us both to fly free and remember the best moments of our friendship. I apologize for my hate towards you and your family. I apologize for the grudge I held against you for almost two years before allowing God to transform my heart to forgive you and then myself. I pray this letter finds you well and your son is thriving and becoming the young man of God that I know you will raise him to be. I pray that even if you don't respond to this letter and decide to never forgive me that God will soften your heart to forgive me one day; although we may never speak again; if I was to ever see you, no matter where I am, I will show love towards you because that is what love truly is. It's putting another person's life before your own. Your life matters to me and had I decided to end it based on an irrational and immature argument I would have to suffer with those consequences for the rest of my life. Most importantly your son would not be raised by an amazing mother and Woman of God I KNOW YOU are!! I pray that we can all learn and grow from what happen that night and close this chapter and allow our hearts to heal and extend Grace to one another for allowing our friendship to fall apart after just one night. God is so much more powerful than one night and if He can extend grace and mercy to us every day for our horrible and sometimes disgusting actions, surely, we can love others. How can we say we love Him if we don't?

With much love, respect and trust for you I hope you accept this letter of forgiveness.

Sincerely,

Shiarnice Taylor

<u>**Scars**</u>

It's amazing how God created this corpse to heal itself.
 Skin folding over into itself to keep one from
 Bleeding. It's the perfect
combination of pain and
forgiveness. Our bodies are
modeled after God's
love for us. It's miraculous
how broken bones mend and weld themselves
back together. It's the exact replica of watching
snakes shedding their skin only to recreate itself
back over again. The skin reminds me of distensible
leather on the inside of a pair of Christian Louboutin shoes;
 our soles are worn out, but our bodies don't stop mending.
Our bodies don't stop forgiving itself. Repeatedly
it's the perfect satire like watching a screen play of a
cheating human being stretching and stuffing a body
with food, stress, sweat and sin and
yet we watch our bodies that God created heal itself
 repeatedly. Marvelous miracles! A love-hate relationship
sometimes called a situation-ship and our scars narrate
the story line of carrying burdens too long, our
insecurities are proven innocent by plastic surgery
 and we take the stand committing perjury against

our own flesh. Sinful scars are hidden behind, tucked

in shirts and tummy tucks and liposuctions suck the

 life out of us because we keep striving for perfection

when God has already given us this body that He

created as a perfect vessel. If our bodies aren't an

 example to you that there is a God. Then you keep

believing that people are miraculously healed

from an imaginary source.

Scars on my body tell tales of disobedience,

yellow flags on the playing field of my body

defiled by mistakes and heartaches that could

 have been avoided in the first place. My scars

 under my eyes are a result of toiling too much,

laboriously stressing over things, I couldn't control

and anxious heart and feet that moved too quickly.

 I was so ready to eat that I devoured my own appetite,

leaving behind burns from pots that weren't handled

 carefully because humans are greedy and inpatient.

Scars once dominated a depressed mindset which

 made an appearance on the stage of my wrist

dancing with blood shadowing my insecurities

But this body that God created renewed first a

new proven testimony that I was enough to God

and even to myself and new skin miraculously

appeared, placing bandages over bondage,

releasing me a body that didn't know how to forgive itself.

Scar tissue is a result a body trying to forgive

 itself for sins it knowingly committed whether

you're healing or hurting, God created your body

to forgive you and your scars are a result of his Grace!

Letter to my Best friend

To call you my best friend is an insult. In fact, it is an understatement to you; because you are more than a BFF, more than a friend, more than words that can describe who you have been to me. You are my sister! You may question why I would even need to write you an apology letter, but the truth is you deserve a lot more. A letter does not suffice so I pray that my actions always reflect to you what you mean to me. When we met during our sophomore year at Sam Houston State University singing in Soul Lifters Gospel Choir I maybe had a glimpse of who you were and who you would become to me. You were always quiet, introverted, kind, a giving and beautiful spirit. From you agreeing to allow your car to be the permanent rode car for all Soul Lifters engagements that were outside of Huntsville, your generosity preceded you. We went from knowing each other during those times where we communicated very little to communicating a lot more upon my junior to senior year when me and my 8th grade best friend fell out. You became a permanent force in my life. You became, and I am ashamed to say this, but my back up friend. The friend I called on when I was having trouble with my main friends. Someone to confide in and often party with. When I was having relationship problems you became my person of solace and understanding. I owe you what should be the sincerest apologies out of all my letters because in my honesty I can truly say I didn't treat you like the friend you were to me. I treated you like a bible stowed away on a bookshelf only to be used on Easter Sunday and Mother's Day. I'm still repulsed by how selfish I am sometimes when often you are better to me than I am to myself. Upon graduation you became more to me. A spirit that was calming to all the chaos I felt in my mind, body and spirit. You were a place of direction when I was so lost and although often we were probably lost together you never passed judgement, allowing me to be myself until I found God. You accepted me even when you knew I wasn't right. You called me often, answered my text messages while I ignored flaming red flags all over the place of jealous friends who eventually tried to end me. I knew and know now you would never end me nor hurt me. There is always so much truth that proceeds out of the mouth of a drunken spirit. I know now that I am a selfish person, I am an It's-all-about-me and "I'm-running- the- show-type" of person. My spirit is ugly at times and my soul is raggedy and tow up from the floor up and, yet you still call me friend. You loved me on purpose, with intent and you never asked for any apology, but I'll give it anyway. I apologize for making you leftovers when you should have been the main course, not an appetizer because when I am around you your laughter and friendship fills me up. They say that your friends are a reflection of who you truly are. Well as my friend you are a reflection of patience, joy, laughter, peace, acceptance and I don't know who "they is", but they never accounted for how messed up I am because we are opposites. I am abrasive, often a pessimist, and it's difficult for me to laugh because of how serious I am. But you see me. You see the real me. The me that's neurotic, goofy, a mind of chaos, but also a spirit striving for peace and I know I can tell you anything and everything. I know God placed you in my life for a reason and I apologize for not seeing that reason a lot sooner until it mattered. After losing what I thought was my whole world of friendship in New Orleans, you were here back in Houston waiting to embrace me and pick me back up and it might have not mattered sooner until it mattered when it mattered. The timing of our friendship couldn't be more on purpose than now. You are my now-friend and I pray my future-friend. My sister, I love you and I pray you accept my apology for often challenging you to be better, to do better to step outside of your box and be great mentally, spiritually, emotionally and physically. Accept my apology for all the facial expressions that I cannot seem to hold in. For all the people I will want to hurt for you because they mean you no good. For all the moments we will make together where I will embarrass you to make you better. Just know that I will hold onto to more than ice water for you and all your secrets and promise from this day to hold near and dear to my heart and I promise to never give you advice that I would never take myself. I pray that one day we will both be married attending each other's wedding that I'll be your maid of honor and you mine. That our children will play together and that we can laugh until we are chocolate wasted while pregnant getting fat and full off of each other's love and laughter. I'll babysit for you any day.

You're more than a BFF,

Sincerely your sister in Christ and in life,

Shiarnice Taylor

Forgiving Circumstances

The Poet I Never Dated

As a rule of thumb, I normally never date poets nor artists for that matter, but for many reasons I liked you. I first came onto the poetry scene in 2011 fresh out of a collegiate slam world and I reeked of being an amateur. What I call a street slam, I was used to a more academic and formal style of slamming; I hated slams, but nonetheless they helped bring out the rawness in all poets writing for the sake of competition does something to an artist. It makes us more competitive bringing out pain, laughter, life, family, catastrophic events and controversial topics. I first saw you at Secret Word Café the first poetry spot where I had my feature. I noticed you were older than me; more seasoned on the mic and always seemed to get 3rd or 4th place in every slam you were in. You were one of the dopest poets to me. I had always wondered about who you were and how old you were. Nothing prepared me for the impact you would leave on me when we began to converse in 2016. Nearly almost 6 years later I noticed you began liking my posts and pictures on Facebook which led to liking more pictures and emoji's on Instagram. In my season of singleness, I couldn't understand why you were liking so many pictures and sending me heart eye emoji's (I was never good at catching on when men flirt with me). Nonetheless I enjoyed it so much it sparked a conversation between us where I learned that you had been playing basketball overseas and traveling the world doing things you loved and that amazed me. The more we conversed the more I became fascinated with your love for Christ and your personal testimony of how a car accident left you wheelchair bound for the rest of your life. You told me how you lost your legs, and that was as vulnerable as I thought you could get. Then you became more intriguing when you expressed to me that your tragic accident increased your faith in God and how you felt that if God hadn't humbled you and took you through depression you wouldn't have understood that there was life even after losing limbs. You went on to say that losing your legs created an opportunity for you to play wheelchair basketball and travel the world. I was fascinated with your testimony and your ability to still have faith and trust God through all of it. Our conversations continued; your spiritual maturity and vast knowledge of the bible made me want to learn more, want to study God's word more. We debated quite often (but I explained I don't argue logistics of the bible).

Our discussions became even more heated. Eventually fascination and curiosity turned into interrogations about whether I believed once a person becomes saved if they could lose their salvation. My answer was simply I didn't know. In my experience of bible studies and my own personal biblical studies in addition to joining a new church and discovering new things about Christianity I truly couldn't answer the question. My instinct told me to say yes so, I replied "Yes, I do believe one can lose their salvation if they backslide and stop following Christ". I now know I should've thought about my answer a lot longer. What was an informative debate turned into accusations that I would never be a good mother if I was planning on teaching my children that they could lose their salvation. The question I asked was how does answering that question or lack of understanding the answer to that question call into question what type of mother I would become or my character? I became highly upset even more as my church and the leaders within my church were attacked and called into question about what they were teaching me and why didn't I know the answer to these questions. He stated, "You should question your church that you are attending if you believe that you can lose your salvation." In return I became deeply upset and a never-ending argument started. He revealed to me several scriptures such as John 10:28-29 (ESV) "I give them eternal life, and no one will snatch them out of my hand. My Father, who has given them to me, is greater than all, and no one is the able to snatch them out of the Father's hand." I didn't trust his interpretation nor his explanation of this scripture. In addition, I did not trust his ability to lead me in the direction of which God would reveal this answer to me. I decided to consult Young Adult leaders within the new ministry I had joined on our Group Me chat and found that in fact he was correct. Once we as Christians accept Jesus Christ as our Lord and Savior, believe He died on the cross, was resurrected and he rose on the third daily truly we are forever saved and there is nothing we could ever do to lose our salvation. How remarkable how God sees fit to allow us to keep our salvation no matter what we have done. This Poet that I never dated and would never date, taught me how immature I was at the time within my Christian faith. How like many people I had so much more work to do for Christ, so much more of His word that I needed to learn and hide in my heart. He taught me that my emotions during that time ruled in my life more than I allowed God to control them, that my reactions were primarily based on fear. A fear of being abandoned or never loved. A fear of never having the opportunity again to talk about marriage, children, what season we would get married in and how soon it would occur? A fear of having to one day possibly choose between two people I love. I don't regret never dating you because had we dated and gotten married I never would have understood what it's like to date God. Thank you for understanding what a messed up, confused, emotionally imbalanced, baby Christian I was. You helped me grow and gave me true convictions about wanting to know more about God and His word. Forgive me for my lack of understanding of the word at the time, for my inability to control my emotions, and allow God to control my emotions. Forgive me for my indecisiveness and lack of trust in God. Forgive me for making decisions to have conversations with you regarding a future in marriage that were based primarily on the fear of never getting married. I now understand that God has allowed me to be single for a reason and there is so much more growth the more I spend with Him. Every day I become the person I desire in a spouse. Forgive me for shutting the door of love and friendship and not loving you like Christ loved us, for harboring resentment for you from how things ended. I welcome you to open the door again my brother in Christ. If you ever need to know what God's love looks like I promise to be a better representation of Him next time.

<u>Emotional Equilibrium</u>

I hate commercials!!

How they seem to conveniently

Make their way into regular scheduled.

Programming even when listening

To Pandora or watching YouTube videos,

 because someone

Paid for a commercial they find

It so convenient to take away

Minutes of your enjoyment

Fun filled entertainment

That I don't feel I should have to

Stop because someone

Conveniently wanted to advertise a product, a business,

An event, special occasions they make me sick!!

Before you came and interrupted the best TV show

In life I had plans to celebrate my birthday without

You!! Plans to invite friends who aren't just place holders

Or bookmarks for me to return to pages already read.

I had plans to get my hair done gets my nails done and drive

Around the city allowing the wind to dry the paint

What did we do before commercials?

Before PSA's where people had to interrupt their lives

For unhappy moments that they never get back.

I hate unintentional surprises that stop traffic

 interrupting the flow of a woman at peace with being single

A woman with no intention of dating anyone except herself and God

You must thrive off showing up unannounced,

mooch off moments where you can watch a woman's heart take screeching halt's praying that she won't have a heart attack

because you indulge in watching her heart do this over and over again!!

I hate small talk!!

What do you want exactly?

What was so important that you had to change the channel when you saw I was watching scandal!!

When you saw I had reached emotional equilibrium you changed

The pace conveniently right on time for you but taunting and teachable moment for me

You still haven't changed!!

You timing is still off

Still late to things you weren't invited to and still early to things that you haven't grown into.

Yet you know how to make me change by just picking up the phone to say happy birthday!!

I guess convenience is like pain. It's relative and depending on who you talk to its promising

So, I guess I should pay attention to the product you're selling during this commercial

It could be a gimmick, or it could be fruition

But my spirit says it's only a fling to get me to go back to that old thing that we both know is a day late and a commercial payment short so back to scheduled programming

My show

My song

My life is on and I don't want to miss any parts of it!!

Fear

There is nothing to fear but fear itself

There is nothing to fear but fear itself

There is nothing to fear but fear itself

I can imagine if I keep saying this enough like Dorothy in The Wizard of Oz

I'll be darted across an open sky to a land where you can cast all your cares and worries

Onto the Great Oz and I would be a cowardly lion asking for courage just to fight fear to get out of

What the tin man wishes for my brain praying I won't go insane I just want to go home!

So, I click my heels and say 3 times, "There is nothing to fear but fear itself" (3x)

Am I out of my head yet?

Can you imagine if time went backwards? If clocks read the same time when you looked 5 minutes ago?

How about 5 hours ago?

I was just sitting at work waiting to go home waiting to clock out, but I

keep reliving clocking in

It's like rowing a boat backwards, like seeing an hour glass empty

itself onto the same side, like rain drops descending into an open sky,

like watching foliage reattach itself back to trees in fall we take leaps

forward and spring backwards. It's like watching a waterfall evaporate into its source. The source is fear, the emotion is afraid, the action is run like putting a revolver next to the shot gun. This anxiety is not fun.

It's war against oneself and an outside spirit, an Angel of Crazy that gives you every ounce of fear that holds more weight than my soul put a boulder in my brain and watch it sink my self-esteem Anxiety killed every dream and every shot I ever had at happiness, Watch God resurrect my soul and collect the remnants of what makes me whole after aversions have contaminated my mold.

It's like watching a shoreline run back to the sea

It's like bathing in regret and tanning in shame. Whatever you do don't get your hopes up because they say it never goes away

But my God is a bulldozer of self-doubt and a savior of sin, a curator of courage

He's a whisperer in my ear silently shouting peace be still!!

He's a crossing guard between the streets of my heart and my mind he stops the cerebral stress of my brain, only allowing hope to enter a troubled space

Jesus is my safe space

I've tried B.F. Skinnering my way through; but negative reinforcements seemed inoperative to an operant condition. My condition can't be treated the same as teaching a dog to salivate after treats.

My condition is not congruent to dropping a mouse in a maze to go after treats.

You can't drown out the sounds of misery with classical music, you can write to get bad thoughts out of your head, replace negative thoughts with a positive truth, equate fear to anxiety with cognitive behavioral therapy all day long.

 The truth is your mind still tells you to run.

There is something about a brain that can never be silenced. How do I quiet this orchestra of dismay?

I was never good enough.

I will never be good enough.

He will never be good enough.

He is not enough.

There is nothing to fear, but fear itself.

There is nothing to fear, but fear itself.

There is nothing to fear; but I think Paul said it better than FDR when he wrote, "For God hath not given us the spirit of fear; but of power, and of love, and a sound mind."

I wrote until my fingers bled, was conditioned by a response to establish a treaty with my pain but I say to my therapist it's not what you could do or even I to destroy what you diagnosed as (GAD (Generalized Anxiety Disorder). You were only able to put a band aid on a dilapidated soul; but when I gave GAD to GOD I was finally made whole.

He was always good enough.

He will always be good enough.

He is more than good enough.

God is enough!!!

<u>**Single**</u>

I enjoy being single because I know that God didn't create for myself.

When I'm lonely I remember that God didn't create me to be all one so surely. He didn't create me to be alone.

 I was created to be a part of a body and when I think of my body I gotta take It back to Genesis.

Because I was created from something else, better yet someone else, Adam.

Not to be confused with the atom that made up particles of our bodies which were still not created individually it takes Adam to make Eve and you and me see we are created in God's image.

I enjoy being single because it teaches me about patience

that if I get to know myself more than I get to know you then

I'll know myself so well that now I have more time to focus on

getting to know you and because I know me and the God that created

we I can already tell you that He didn't create you for me.

Being single gives me a clarity and confirmation that I don't have to ask God for because I know if He created me then He has me

right where I'm supposed to be. If He wanted me married I would

already be.

If He wanted me with children, He would have already intervened

 on my behalf blessing me in the midst of my sin;

 but He sent His son to die for all my past and future transgressions.

If it's a blessing after committing a sin I can't say I'd be proud of it.

 It's not like seeing a rainbow after the rain, but even after all the pain

His covenant reigns.

I enjoy being single because I get to date God.

Which means I'm engaged to my faith, which means if my faith ever

wavers and I get into my feelings versus my faith my man,

God can bring me back to my faith and put my feelings in place.

Checkmate!

I enjoy being single because I'm tired of hearing women

complaining about unequally yoked men that they're dating

and they're trying to make it work.

They are patiently waiting for something that they know

 he won't wait for.

They are tired of getting stood up for bible study and

Sunday school, hoping and praying that something the pastor will say

will make them choose to be saved today.

I enjoy being single because I'm tired of hearing

brothers brag about how sisters is loose and ain't got

no standards; but they claiming they love her when

love is caring about another person more than yourself. So instead of

recognizing that sister aint just loose she is lost, they're choosing to

stay never once choosing to value the person over the property.

That's why I'm single;

 because I never want to have meaningless arguments with people

 who ain't worth wasting my breathe on death when I could be

choosing to breathe life into my situations.

I'm single because situation-ships aint hip no more.

No, I'm sorry the new terminology is lit. They aint lit no more.

 I'd rather be at peace than to be pacing bathrooms floors waiting on

positive results from a pregnancy test that I wouldn't need if I just

knew how to be obedient and play my position by staying single!!

I enjoy being single because my tests are from God

not from man and I ain't gotta worry about a Plan B or STD

when he/she decides they want to up and leave me with a baby or even

worse.

I'd rather be single than deal with that heartache

and it may make your heart break to know that

I've decided to wait until marriage to have sex.

Yes, I've been single going on 3 years because of it;

but I know where my help and my health comes from.

So, I've chosen heaven over heartbreaks.

I've chosen healing over headaches and joy over jump-off's.

If you being single can't seem to wait and believe that what you need is more important than what God says we both need which is eternal salvation, then I guess you love yourself more than you Love God!

I'm single because it's right where God wants me and I ain't going nowhere until He moves me.

<u>**4 Give me 4 Eva**</u>

Forever is a mighty long time; but that's how long

I am requesting that you give me.

For all the times we will argue about where

Our kids will go to school, about where we will attend church

About where we live, whether or not we are ready to buy a house.

Forever, for every time I undermine your leadership and decide to make

 My own decision, for every consequence our family will suffer from

Because of

My disobedience to follow God's headship. I ask for forgiveness in advance.

For all the times you will ask me to do something that I don't want to do.

All the times I'll do it just to appease you.

For all the times you will make decisions without me. How

Our lack of communication will reflect the flaws in our children.

Our imperfect of a perfect marriage we will have.

For all the times I want to leave you but can't because we took vows

Under the covenant of God replicating God's love for us and the church.

We have entered the ultimate sacrifice with one another dying to ourselves daily;

And bearing (yes, God forgive us, we bear) sometimes the cross of marriage.

The shackles of what seems like a never-ending battle, what seems like prison I ask in advance to God that you forgive us.

When our marriage is not enough to save our family.

Forgive us when we fail each other, and I stop submitting to my husband and he stops submitting to you and our children are straying because we chose not to align ourselves in perfect symmetry.

Forgive us for the people who you knew we would be in the first place.

I forgive you, my spouse, my love, my life for making decisions that will impact our family.

Those decisions that shake the brink of our financial stability.

For decisions that are truly in sickness and in health when you may choose to have your Mother in Law come and stay with us.

When you choose whose family, we visit for the holidays

When you choose to have me stay home and retire my career, degrees, and all my hard work just to make more time for our family

I will hate you for it!

But I will love you for forgiving me nonetheless because my human flesh sometimes can't comprehend pleasing anyone but myself

And I won't make excuses for how complacent I became in my singleness to justify my selfishness to you

I just hope that you accept my apology in advance for the flawed woman I am, and the flawed woman you will marry, because one thing I've learned is that I won't come wrapped with a bow of perfection

But I'll try my hardest to wrap my heart in grace for you and wrap my mind in mercy for you and to love you like Christ loved us and if I must spend forever showing you how to love me and how I should love you even in our flawed fatalities I'd rather forgive you and lose you than to never forgive you and let go!

Forgive me Forever!!

Forgiving Myself

"Forgive yourself, forgive him, Forgive It"- Nikki Taplin

I remember this statement being the

Very thing I needed to hear when I called my sister (my accountability partner)

And advised her of the sin I had just committed. The very sin that kept me bound for so many years, the very sin that she called me and warned me not to commit during a date on the day before.

I remember how empty I felt, how depressed I felt.

How I just wanted to wallow and drag my sorrow around like a sack of sin.

A load that I carry every day. I can't seem to get away from my flesh.

Truth is no one can!!

I can't seem to get away from my own love language of touch and the biggest lesson learned this year for me has been the reality that I WILL ALWAYS STRUGGLE WITH THE ISSUE OF WANTING TO BE AND FEEL WANTED! I WILL ALWAYS STRUGGLE WITH MY FLESH!! I WILL ALWAYS STRUGGLE WITH WANTING TO BE

TOUCHED, HUGGED, LOVED, KISSED, MISSED, PHYSICAL INTIMACY IS MY WEAKNESS.

Now I know you may be wondering why would she even be willing to reveal this? Well it's for the exact reason that I'm so transparent about everything else in my life. Someone; and it could even be you that STRUGGLES WITH THIS SAME THING!

I'm reminded of a bible study class in which another lesson was learned this year. "Some things in this life you will die still trying to escape from." "Some things in this life you will always struggle with." The reality is only GOD CAN DELIVER YOU FROM THOSE THINGS!! STOP TRYING TO FIX IT YOURSELF!

For all the mistakes I have made in my life, I forgive myself.

For all the wrongs I could not make right, I forgive myself.

For all the times I doubted God could bring me through, I forgive myself.

All the times I was ungrateful.

All the times I disrespected my mother and father.

All the times I used my body as a weapon of mass destruction, I forgive me!

For all the times I used my body as a human toilet I forgive myself!

For all the times I ended up with "egg on my face" from stupid immature mistakes I still make, I forgive me!

For those times when I wasn't there for my family, I forgive myself!!

For all the times I wasn't there for friends, I forgive myself!!

For all the times I curse and complain.

For all the times I was stupid enough to believe I could change him, I forgive myself!!

For the time I thought I was strong enough in my celibacy and underestimated my strength, I forgive myself.

For putting myself in compromising situations making it nearly impossible to make a way of escape, I forgive myself!!

I forgive me because God forgives me and though it doesn't give me permission to ignore God and do what I want, it is necessary to move on and become better. It is necessary to know that salvation wipes

EVERY SIN CLEAN!

I AM CLEAN, AND I FORGIVE ME!

Forgiving God

Letter to God

You say God is God He doesn't need to be forgiven so why are you writing this?

I say true God is God and He doesn't need our forgiveness!

But I say how about I want God to know how much I love Him and in order to do that I have to tell Him I forgive Him!!

This is a letter of gratitude to the one and only God I serve.

I saved this letter for last; because God, You mean that much to me!!

In times where I fell from grace and blamed You; You were right there ready with open arms to embrace me.

If I had to apologize for all I've done this letter would be over a billion pages long and You didn't ask for my apology you asked for my repentance.

I want to start with blaming You for my father's absence. Blaming You for allowing me to grow up in an environment with an absent father and a stepfather who abused me and my mother most of my life. Lord I'm sorry for not understanding that generational sins do exist.

That I inherited sin and because of that broken families were a result of other mistakes and I blamed You for that.

I want to thank you for my absent father, because without him being gone I would not have been able to appreciate You. I would not have found You and understand that this entire time I was searching for the love of a father in men who didn't even share my blood;

because Lord You were my blood and You shed Your blood for me.

Lord oftentimes I blamed You for placing me in a job that I now hate.

A job that has taken so much out of me. I was once compassionate, loving, kind, always smiling and this job has taken blood, sweat, tears, pain, stolen my joy at times, and made me cold.

I blamed You for giving me a glimpse of sunlight; an inkling of hope that I would get out earlier this year. I blamed You for taking that Federal job away from me. My dreams, my hopes, my aspirations of going to law school.

I'm sorry, Lord, for I realize that not only do You have a plan for Your provision, but You see the bigger picture. I have made You so small and made myself so big.

How dare I?

You have revealed so much to me about the plans You have for me and even still I blamed You for not bringing my husband and children to me sooner.

I'm sorry, Lord, for I know now that there were so many things I needed to learn and still learning to be able to appreciate truly what it would mean to be a wife and mother. I now understand that had You given me a husband earlier and children that those things would consume me, and I would turn them into idols and You, Lord, don't deserve that.

I want You to know God that You are THE LOVE OF MY LIFE.

When I fall asleep at night I feel, You holding me like nobody ever could.

Like no man will ever be able to.

You hold me like You mean that You love me.

When my anxiety seems to get the best of me and I feel like I can't breathe I feel you breathing for me, grieving for me.

No parent likes to see their child suffer and I know You hear and see me when I do.

I know it's necessary and I want you to know that I thank you for the pain, the stress, the headaches because they bring me right back to YOU!!

YOU ARE ALL THE ONLY ONE THAT CAN ALWAYS BRING ME TO TEARS IN AN INSTANT WHEN I THINK OF ALL YOU'VE DONE FOR ME. I remember that you even created my tears; EVERYTHING BRINGS ME BACK TO YOU.

YOU ARE THE LOVE OF MY LIFE AND IF I HAD A MILLION OF ME TO SAY THANK YOU THERE WOULD STILL BE ONLY ONE YOU!!

FORGIVE ME, GOD, FOR ALWAYS BLAMING YOU!!

<u>H.A.R.V.E.Y.</u>

Melodies of rain on tin roofs use to rock me into a deep sleep;

But now sounds like alternative music nails hitting sheetrock under my feet.

I think it's now called Heavy Metal.

Where precipitation now inundates my eardrums. It seems to never stop

Raining I've prayed for mercy for over 5 days now. I used to see rainbows as blessings;

But I can only see rainbows when it stops. When will it ever stop raining, Lord?

Lord, how much praise will it take for us to reach the precipice of the end of this precipitation?

 I can't remember the last time I knew what it felt like not to have my heart race. Can you tell me when the palpitations will stop?

Is this because of all the mistakes that we as Christians make?

When will my neighborhoods stop looking like a lake?

When will boatloads of blessings deliver us out of this mess? When will the name Harvey stop playing this same song like a broken record like it's on repeat. Lord, when can we get some relief?

When will I get to hear my families voice again, because we are divided by peninsula wards and last time I tried to get to my mama's house I saw tank trucks reminding me of 3rd world misery.

Pardon me Lord for questioning You but I've never seen refrigerators used as boats and I never seen desperation look like folks breaking into churches just to find their breakthrough

 I ain't never seen the tips of roofs look like icebergs.

Skyscrapers submerged, Lord, what are you trying to tell us?

 Is there a scripture or chapter in Revelations that we missed? Did I fall asleep on a sermon entitled

"Caution turn around don't drown"

I'm just wondering how I could have avoided this?

Were our hazard lights too dim for You to see us?

Did we depend too much on FEMA from past devastations? Forget to pay our tides but added GAP insurance to our premium I'm just trying to figure out if we forgot to bless our food over my families' dinner table?

 For you drop us from premium to basic cable

How right when it seemed that none of us could get it right you took discrimination and turned it into devastation

It got it worse Lord before it got better!!

And the Lord answered…

When will your praise match the amount of precipitation that reigned over your city?

When will you see me the God that has reigned forever over your city?

You left me to focus on social injustices.

You focused more on the blessing than the one who blessed.

Now your whole world is a complete wreck and I'm here to clean up your mess.

Harvey is just the beginning of a Nation under God coming together to Heal All Rivalry so that Victory from God can enlighten You!